Guess Who
Dives

Sharon Gordon

BENCHMARK BOOKS

MARSHALL CAVENDISH
NEW YORK

Did you see me jump
out of the water?

The ocean is my home.

I am not a fish.

I need to breathe air, just like you.

I swim to the top.

I breathe through my *blowhole*.

Then I dive back down.

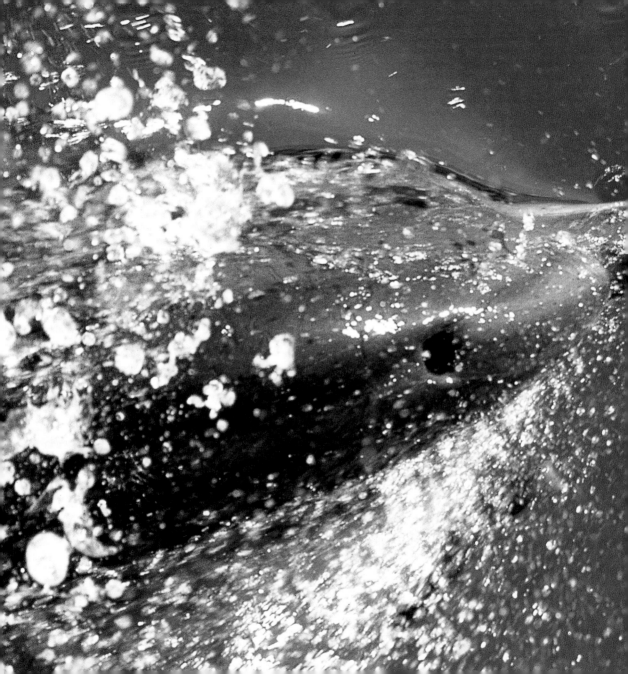

My skin is smooth.

It helps me swim fast.

I travel in a group called a *pod*.

Our babies are called *calves*.

I slap my tail on the water if there is danger.

Everyone swims away quickly.

My eyes see well in the water.

I can also "see" by making sounds.

I send out clicking sounds.

The sounds come back
to me.

The sounds tell me how big something is.

They also tell me where it is.

I like to eat all kinds of fish.

I catch them with my sharp teeth.

But I would not hurt you.

You can swim with me!

Who am I?

I am a dolphin!

Who am I?

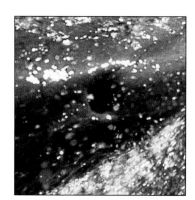

blowhole

eye

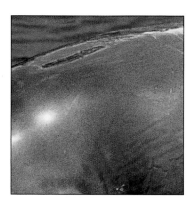

skin

tail

teeth

Challenge Words

blowhole (blow-hole)
A hole at the top of a dolphin's head used for breathing.

calves (kavs)
Baby dolphins.

pod
A group of dolphins.

Index

Page numbers in **boldface** are illustrations.

About the Author

Sharon Gordon has written many books for young children. She has also worked as an editor. Sharon and her husband Bruce have three children, Douglas, Katie, and Laura, and one spoiled pooch, Samantha. They live in Midland Park, New Jersey.

With thanks to Nanci Vargus, Ed.D. and
Beth Walker Gambro, reading consultants

Benchmark Books
Marshall Cavendish
99 White Plains Road
Tarrytown, New York 10591-9001
www.marshallcavendish.com

Library of Congress Cataloging-in-Publication Data

Gordon, Sharon.
Guess who dives / by Sharon Gordon.
p. cm. — (Bookworms: Guess who)
Includes index.
Summary: Clues about the dolphin's physical characteristics, behavior,
and habitat lead the reader to guess what animal is being described.
ISBN 0-7614-1554-8
1. Dolphins—Juvenile literature. [1. Dolphins.] I. Title.
II. Series: Gordon, Sharon. Bookworms: Guess who.

QL737.C432G673 2003
599.53'2—dc21
2002155812

Photo Research by Anne Burns Images

Cover photo by: *Animals, Animals*/Lewis S. Trusty

The photographs in this book are used with permission and through the courtesy of: *Animals, Animals*:
pp. 1, 23, 29 (right) Gerard Lacz; p. 3 Lewis S. Trusty; pp. 11, 28 (lower) D. Lee; pp. 15, 29 (left) James Watt. *Visuals Unlimited*:
pp. 5, 13 Dave B. Fleetham; p. 7 Mark E. Gibson; pp. 9, 28 (upper left) James D. Watt; p. 21 Hal Beral. *Peter Arnold*:
pp. 17, 27, 28 (upper right) Gerard Lacz; p. 19 Jeffrey L. Rotman; p. 25 Kelvin Aitken.

Series design by Becky Terhune

Printed in China
1 3 5 6 4 2